D0753771

NAVAJO RUGS

- past, present & future -

by

GILBERT S. MAXWELL

In collaboration with

EUGENE L. CONROTTO

Published by
BEST-WEST PUBLICATIONS
P. O. Box 757
Palm Desert, California

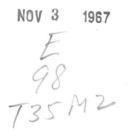
PRINTED BY DESERT PRINTERS, INC. PALM DESERT, CALIFORNIA

CONTENTS

FOREWORD

This book concerns itself with the origin of the different types of Navajo rugs, with suggestions on how and where to buy, and with their care. New historical notes were added to facts previously known. The history of the Navajo People has been sketchily depicted and then only as it concerns their weaving. I have not gone into the general economic situation of the Navajo, even though weaving has been an important factor as far as the women are concerned. Trying to tell the story of the rugs and blankets has been enough of a problem without going into these other phases.

To Eugene L. Conrotto, former publisher of the Desert Magazine, for his help in putting together the first draft of this book.

To Tom Bahti, of the Bahti Shop, Tucson, Arizona, go my thanks for his helpful criticisms and suggestions, and for writing the introduction.

To Paul Huldermann, of the House of Six Directions, Scottsdale, Arizona, my thanks for editing and suggesting many fine points.

To James Price, of Price's All Indian Shop, Old Town Albuquerque, New Mexico, thanks for letting me photograph some of his rugs.

To my wife, Dorothy Field Maxwell, go many thanks for prodding and suggesting, for her research, rewriting and for her help in every way possible.

GILBERT S. MAXWELL

Farmington, New Mexico
October, 1963

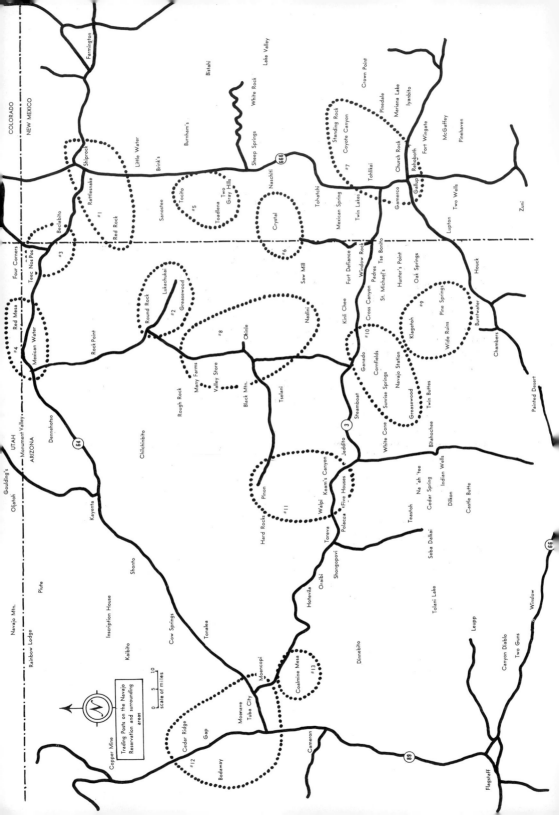

LIST OF ILLUSTRATIONS

For the purpose of easier comparison, all color plates are gathered in the center of this book, even though the text references are scattered throughout the pages.

UNM-MC, following descriptive lines under the photographs, signifies that the item is part of the Maxwell Collection in the Anthropological Museum of the University of New Mexico, Albuquerque, New Mexico.

CHARTS

INTRODUCTION

The knowledge gained by the author in twenty years of collecting and sixteen years of dealing in Navajo textiles has gone into this book. The result is a highly readable account that will appeal to both the serious collector and the interested amateur.

This multi-purpose book provides a concise and extremely well-illustrated historical summary of old blankets and a comprehensive survey of contemporary weaving. For the person who can't tell warp from weft there are invaluable tips on buying, collecting and the care and feeding of Navajo rugs. The life of a Navajo rug is traced, step by step, from sheep to salesman.

Much has been written about Navajo textile arts but this is the first book by an individual directly involved in the economics of the craft. Too often in a discussion of arts and crafts the intrusion of the word *economics* is regarded in a negative light. Yet this is one of the most important aspects of the craft. Weaving has always been a prime trade item among the Navajo. The same laws of economics that caused the craft to flourish will also be responsible for its eventual death.

Fortunately, the dollars and cents phase of Navajo rugs is not neglected and Mr. Maxwell is well qualified to write on this subject. During the past sixteen years he has bought and sold a total of 38,272 rugs.

Equally welcome is the information regarding the hours of labor that go into producing a rug.

Through a series of coincidences, I acquired, in 1951, my first Navajo blanket of historic interest. Less than a month passed when a genial gentleman appeared at my door, and said, "I've heard you have an early Navajo blanket and I wonder if I might have a look at it." This was my first introduction to Gil Maxwell.

I mention this incident as an acknowledgement of Mr. Maxwell's ability and determination as a collector. Lest it be thought that his tracking down of Navajo textiles was limited to the Southwest it should be stated that many of his finest examples were located in such far-away-places-with-strange-sounding-names as California, Illinois and Virginia.

This thoroughness paid off handsomely in the form of 118 fine specimens of Southwestern weaving, beginning with the earliest dated (1804-05) fragment of a Navajo blanket from Massacre Cave in Canyon del Muerto, Arizona and ending with the last year's prize-winning Two Gray Hills tapestry weave. Not only is each stage in the development of Navajo textiles represented by outstanding examples but also included are samples of other weaving that influenced this craft; the Saltillo blanket of Coahuila, Mexico, Rio Grande textiles, and Pueblo fabrics.

I am pleased to add that the public has ready access to these specimens. Gil Maxwell donated his collection except where noted later, to the Anthropology Museum of the University of New Mexico in Albuquerque, thus completing his original goal of returning to the Southwest significant examples of the Navajo weavers' art.*

TOM BAHTI

Tucson, Arizona
October, 1963.

*An unexpected bonus was obtained with this collection through the happy reunion of the Massacre Cave fragments shown in Photo 1. Obviously a single piece at the time of discovery it was later cut into three parts and each passed from one collector to another. One piece was acquired by the Laboratory of Anthropology in Santa Fe; it was cut from the piece shortly after it was obtained by Mr. Maxwell, in 1951, from the Roe Emery Collection. The third piece was given to the Anthropology Museum of the University of New Mexico in 1955. Since no information was included with this latter item it was catalogued simply as a "fragment of Navajo weaving". It was not until after the Maxwell gift had been received and a comparison made that it was discovered that the pieces were from the same blanket.

T.B.

CHAPTER ONE —

HISTORY

Prior to the coming of the Spaniards to the Desert Southwest, the American Indian tribes in this area (or soon to come into this area) were roughly divided into two types: the farmers, and the raider-huntsmen.

The Pueblos, whose misfortune it would be to play host to the cruel Conquistadores, were farmers. The Navajos (along with their cousins, the Apaches) were raider-huntsmen, forever on the prowl.

As farmers, the Pueblos, among other things, raised cotton, thus contributing directly to their highly developed art of textile weaving. Indeed, the Conquistadores are uncharacteristically generous with praise of the clothing worn by these Indians.[1]

It is significant to the purpose of this book to note that when Coronado's army left Compostela in 1540, bound for the conquest of the Seven Cities of Cibola, his entourage included 5000 sheep. These sheep were the *churro*, the kind used by the peasant people of Spain. The Merino, introduced later to the New World, was then reserved for royalty. These *churro* were scrawny, long-legged and had straight, long wool. This wool needed little preparation for weaving and the sheep needed little care. The wool was practically greaseless and was often a brown color. Sometimes these sheep had four horns, perhaps this was due to inbreeding. Even today we find an occasional four-horned sheep in the northwest section of the reservation.[2]

While the lives of the Indians in New Mexico and northern Arizona would eventually come to be profoundly altered by this lowly beast, the transformation was not an overnight thing. Indian Agents had the idea of importing new kinds of sheep to improve the breed. In 1883 Merino were bought and lent to the Navajo. In 1903 the French Merino, called Rambouillet, were brought in, mainly for meat and marketable wool. Unfortunately, it turned out that the lambs born were too large for the *churro* ewes. Eventually the sheep grew bigger, but the wool was shorter, kinkier and greasier. Navajo women found it hard to clean and almost impossible to spin.₃ Many different types of sheep have been used as experiments, but all seemed to have some faults. The Rambouillet is the principal type of sheep used today on the Navajo Reservation.

Now, while the tide of Europeans was moving northward out of Mexico to engulf the Pueblos in the 16th and 17th centuries, another simultaneous invasion was moving southward out of the Plateau country—the Navajos were on the move. While it is almost a certainty that Coronado and his sheep met no Navajos in the forays of the 1540s, there can be little doubt that a century later the descendants of both the Conquistadores and their livestock began fraternizing with the Navajos.

By the beginning of the 18th century, and after a few bloody protests, the Pueblos had pretty much settled into the Spanish yoke. The Pueblo people acquired sheep from the Spanish and wool, in addition to cotton, occupied the Pueblo looms. But the atmosphere of peace was interrupted ever so often by new invasion forces. The Navajo raiding parties broke into the Pueblos.

It should be emphasized that the Navajo was not merely a stealer of livestock and other material things, he was also as dynamic and adaptable as he was a stealer of ideas. And so, when the setttlement of America snuffed out the raider's way of life, the Navajo had little trouble turning to a new way of life—that of a pastoral nomad—thanks to the Spaniard's horses and sheep. His flocks increased, his contact with the Pueblos gained him the weaver's art, and the natural consequence was the wide-spread production of textiles throughout what was to become *his* Reservation. For the Navajos, the production of textiles meant the production of a commodity that could be traded or sold.

It is not my intention in this book to dwell on minutia. If a date must be assigned to the real start of Navajo weaving, let us accept the 1690s for this.₄ In 1680 the Pueblo Indians sent the Spanish back south by their raids and warfare. Ten years later, in 1690, the Spanish came back in full force and the Pueblo Indians fled to the Gobernador area (east of Farmington, N. Mex.) and stayed in that area for some time. The Pueblos intermarried with the Navajo and there is even one clan of the Navajos called the Jemez clan (from the Jemez Pueblo). It is believed that the Navajo learned the art of weaving from the Pueblo refugees at this time.₅

The first mention of weaving in Spanish records was made in 1706, based on observations of the year previous. The chronicler is Francisco Cuervo y Valdez, Governor of New Mexico, who campaigned against the Navajo in 1705. He wrote: "They (the Navajos) make their clothes of wool and cotton, sowing the latter and obtaining the former from the flocks which they raise.₆

There is a possible explanation for this. Since the Pueblo refugees who made their way into Navajoland had not been in that country for too long a period at that time, it is probable that they continued to plant cotton—and the Navajos quickly imitated them.

The next reference is in testimony taken in Santa Fe in 1743-45 by Governor Codallos y Rabal to aid the Spanish in determining the policy with relation to proposed missions to the Navajos.[7] The people giving the testimony were Spaniards who had been in the Navajo country on campaigns or exploring expeditions (some in the very early 1700s') . Most of these people mention the weaving of wool—particularly black wool—by the Navajos.

By the end of that century (1791) the Governor of New Mexico was able to write to the Viceroy that the Navajos ". . . . dress somewhat better than those of the Pueblos."[8] A few months later, the same writer made mention of the Navajo trade in fabrics. And in 1795, Governor Concha reported that the Navajos ". . . work their wool with more delicacy and taste than the Spaniards."[9]

The period of what we may call the Period of First Weavers lasted about a century and a half, or to 1850. By the time this era came to an end, the simple craft of the Navajo had advanced to the position of a significant craft industry.[10]

The earliest pieces of Navajo weaving which can be definitely dated, and that are still in existence today, come to us from Massacre Cave in Cañon del Muerto.[11] (Photo 1.) Fragments of Navajo weaving dating to 1804-05 when the punitive slaughter took place in the Cañon, were found about 1900 on the skeletal remains of the victims. (See footnote at end of introduction, page 6) . These fragments show a plain stripe pattern in the blanket's designs—a Navajo adaptation of the Pueblo-teacher's style. Therefore, this would lead us to believe that the outstanding qualities of Navajo weaving to 1850 were not so much represented by design variation, but rather by a growth in both quality and quantity.

Navajos who were captured and enslaved by the frontier Spaniards were, naturally, put to work. What better job for idle hands than to weave blankets for the masters. So, from about 1830 to 1860 (or maybe a little later) these slaves were made to weave wearing blankets.[12] These so-called Slave Blankets are exceedingly rare. Parenthetically, some Slave Blankets might have been woven by Spanish slaves at upright looms, as the Navajos also took slaves. All have strong Mexican influences. The Mexican blankets were woven on a horizontal loom and the Navajo blankets were, and are, woven on an upright loom. With the Mexican loom a shuttle (or shuttles) was used to place the weft threads from one edge to another. Pattern colors were inserted during the process, but except for this, the weft threads

1. MASSACRE CAVE FRAGMENTS. (as mentioned in the Introduction). UNM-MC.

went all the way across the warp threads. With the Navajo, instead of putting threads across the face of the work, the slave-weaver would stop as far over and as high as she could comfortably reach. Later she'd move over and finish up the next section, continuing across the width of the blanket. This produced diagonal breaks in the material, known as lazy lines. These lines are not an exclusive province of Slave Blankets, however, for some modern weavers are guilty of lazy line weaving, and we even found some in the Massacre Cave fragments (See Photo 1, diagonal line in upper right light band and upper left light band.)

Approaching full development in mid-century, however, was a distinctive type of blanket—known as a "Chief"—worthy of special notice here.[13] The Chief Blanket was woven by the Navajos for trade or sale to other Indians throughout their trading area. These blankets were not worn by Navajo chiefs, but by "Chiefs" of other tribes because they were the only ones who could afford such luxuries. The Navajos have no actual chiefs. These fine blankets, expertly woven and relatively costly were prestige symbols for Indians and non-Indians alike; they were often presented as gifts to Army commanders. No doubt their popularity had a great deal to do with the development and growing recognition of Navajo weaving. But most important, the Chief Blanket set the pattern for the Navajo textile becoming an "export item"—an economically important factor to these nomad weavers.

The first Chief Blanket featured a simple plain black and white stripe design. (Photo 2) The intermediate-period Chief Blanket went to some rectangles, but still retained a basic black-white stripe motif. (Photo 3)

The later Chief Blanket styles featured corner and center designs as well as the broad stripes. (Photo 4)

Also to be mentioned here is the woman's wearing blanket which differed from the man's wearing blanket (The Chief Blanket), in that it had narrow gray and black stripes instead of the broad black and white bands. Usually the top, bottom and center bands were striped with indigo and had rectangles of bayeta in these stripes. (Photo 5)

The Chief Blanket was the beginning and was for some years part of the so-called Classic Period of Navajo weaving

2. FIRST PHASE CHIEF BLANKET. In this blanket the red is raveled Bayeta and Saxony yarn; blue is indigo dyed handspun; balance is handspun native wool. Circa 1850. UNM-MC.

3. SECOND PHASE CHIEF BLANKET. The red is raveled Bayeta; blue is Indigo dye; balance handspun. Circa 1860. UNM-MC.

4. THIRD PHASE CHIEF BLANKET. The red is raveled Bayeta, blue is Indigo dye, balance handspun. Obtained from the F. H. Douglas Collection. Circa 1870. UNM-MC.

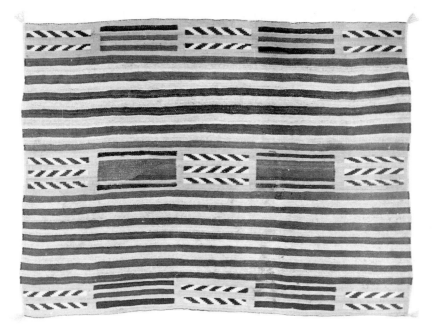

5. WOMAN'S WEARING BLANKET. Commonly called a shoulder blanket. Shows narrow grey and black stripes. Blue is Indigo dye, red and yellow aniline dye, balance is handspun. Circa 1885. Purchased from the Earl H. Morris Collection. UNM-MC.

which lasted from approximately 1850 to approximately 1870. Into this period also fall, above all, what has become known as the Bayeta Blanket. Bayeta (or balleta) — a wool cloth (similar to a loosely woven flannel) was originally made in Manchester, England, and shipped to Mexico via Spain, then moved north over old trade routes into what is now New Mexico and Arizona. It is usually known for its red color (cochineal dye) but it was also made in green and yellow, these latter two colors were rarely used. It was known as baize to the English. The cloth came in bolts and it was easy to unravel the threads and spin them into yarn, usually three-ply, and weave them into their blankets. The Navajo were starved for a good red color for their blankets, and having no way to make a red dye of their own, this bayeta at once became a popular trade item. This valuable red coloring did not come from Spanish uniforms, as it is commonly supposed. In fact, no Navajo blanket of record contains material known to have been in a Spanish uniform, or any other soldier's uniform. The last thing a chinde-fearing Navajo would do would be to touch a dead body, let alone strip it. *Chinde,* in the Navajo language is a ghost or spirit of the deceased, and much to be dreaded.

Thus, with bayeta, the first inroad was made into the use

of handspun yarn, and machine-made bayeta was quickly followed by three-ply yarns, notably Saxony. American flannel soon took the place of the fine imported bayeta and this cloth, had to be shredded, carded and spun for their yarn. Many pieces of later weaving is mistaken for the fine old bayeta. It takes an expert to tell the difference between old bayeta and American flannel.

In 1863, the Navajos were captured, rounded-up and sent to Fort Sumner, New Mexico (also known as the Bosque Redondo). Here they were given machine-made cloth. Velveteen and cotton for the women—to be fashioned into modified copies of the clothing of the pioneer women at the fort. Uunbleached muslin for the men—for their trousers. After their release in 1868 they went back to their reservation, but the use of velveteen blouses for both men and women, the full skirts (and the muslin trousers for the older men and for ceremonial use) can be seen today.[14] (Photo 6)

Around 1880, quality of Navajo weaving banked into a sharp decline. The 10 years from 1880 to 1890 saw the gaudy "eye-dazzlers" replace the finely conceived and design-balanced Bayeta-Saxony Classics. (Photo 17) The aniline dyed Germantown (named after the textile city of Germantown, Pennsylvania) four-ply yarns found their way into the Reservation, and

6. WOMAN'S DRESS, OLD TYPE. Red is raveled Bayeta, blue is Indigo dyed handspun, black is dyed handspun. Woven in two pieces and fastened together, leaving openings for arms and head. Circa 1860. Purchased from Earl H. Morris collection. UNM-MC.

the color starved weavers went on a color jag. (Photo 18). In fact, the Germantown yarns remained highly popular for perhaps 30 years, from 1880 to approximately 1910.[15] Even today we find a few Germantown rugs which belong in the classification just mentioned.

Simultaneously with the Germantown yarn, aniline dyes became a standard commodity on the trading post shelves.[16] But as so often when there seems to be utter confusion and aimlessness in a field of craft a certain incident or series of such incidents causes a sudden regaining of balance and a new chapter develops.

Remember that up to this point all Navajo weaving centered exclusively around the making of blankets that were made for wear and to keep the Navajos warm, or to trade with other Indians. But now in 1890, at the height of the Germantown-aniline dye color splash the decline of Navajo weaving began. Manufactured fabrics continued to infiltrate, and then ready-made clothing and the warm Pendleton blankets came to the Navajos. Navajo weaving of wearing material found itself in conflict with fabricated clothing from the east. The weaving situation of the Navajos was grave indeed and may have become extinct had it not been for one saving circumstance. *More and more people were tossing their Navajo blankets on the floor and using them for rugs.* Traders, at this time (1890-1920) caught on quickly and even though they have been maligned, they probably saved the craft. For they were the ones who insisted that the Navajo weaving style change to a product suitable for use on the floor. They developed a heavier type of weaving with borders instead of stripes. (Photo 19)

And so, the Navajo quietly slipped from blanket to rug weaving, altering the product to better suit its new role. To be sure, the first steps down this new road were more stumble than stride. The first rugs were clumsy things, the yarn poorly cleaned, the wool not even washed to eliminate the grease, the spinning and the dyeing were carelessly done. The workmanship was sometimes shoddy. These were the Pound Blanket days when the trader paid by the pound, and the seldom-lacking customer did likewise. The Navajo caught on quickly. They did not wash the wool to remove grease and dirt, in fact, they pounded sand into the yarn to make the rug weigh more. The good weavers were penalized by this trend, as their work was also paid for by the pound. (Silver workers, too, were penalized at this time, because their work was paid for by the ounce of silver—regardless of their craftsmanship.)

But, as happens so often, a period of degeneration takes its course and then some dedicated souls begin to reverse the tide. Thus, just prior to 1920, a revival of Navajo weaving took its first infant steps. What happened specifically shall be examined later when discussing the different types of Navajo rugs. At this point let us first look at the rug itself and how it is manufactured.

CHAPTER TWO —

HOW THE RUG IS MADE

Two things go into all Navajo rugs: wool and work. A third ingredient, dye, is optional.

Wool, of course, is the chief raw material. If the weaver chooses machine-spun yarn, then her source of supply would be no different than yours: a store. If the weaver uses hand-spun wool, then her source of supply is on the hoof right outside her hogan door.

The long-fibered wool shorn from the back of the sheep is usually earmarked for a rug. (The remaining shorter fibered wool is bagged and sold at the trading post.) The shorn wool is hand-cleaned of burrs and other debris. Then it is washed and dried in the sun.

Carding, with what looks like a pair of curry combs, leaves the wool in long, loose, fluffy rolls. A handful of wool is placed on one of the toothed surfaced carders, and the other is raked across it until the wool fibers are untangled and tend to have a uniform trend in the rolls. It is this hand carding that gives the final product its remarkable strength and wearability for the individual fibers are less apt to be broken when worked by hand. (Photo 7)

Next step—the most important—is to spin the carded wool into threads. The familiar spinning wheel was never used in Navajoland. Instead, a light hand spindle is used. (Photo 8) These devices, which somewhat resemble a miniature ski pole or a long-shafted top, have decided advantages over the spinning wheel. For one thing, the semi-nomadic Indians must travel light; for another, a hand spindle allows the weaver latitude in when and where she can work—while tending the flock, seated in the shade of a tree, gossiping with visiting relatives, in the hogan, in town while her husband is getting a tire fixed.

The spindle is manipulated with the right hand; the wool with the left. A strip of carded wool is twisted around the top of the spindle; then a twirl of the spindle combined with a tug on

7. CARDER

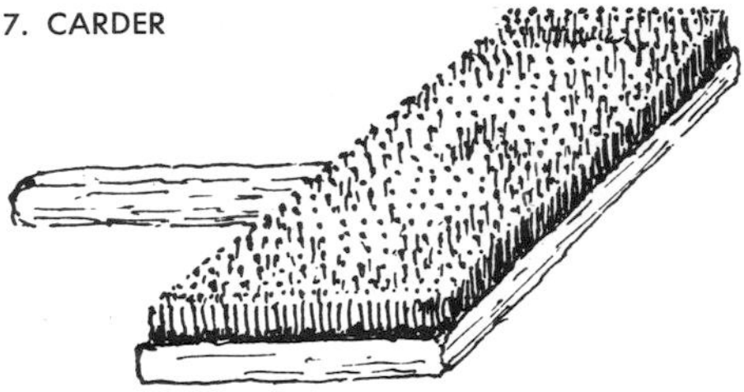

8. SPINDLE

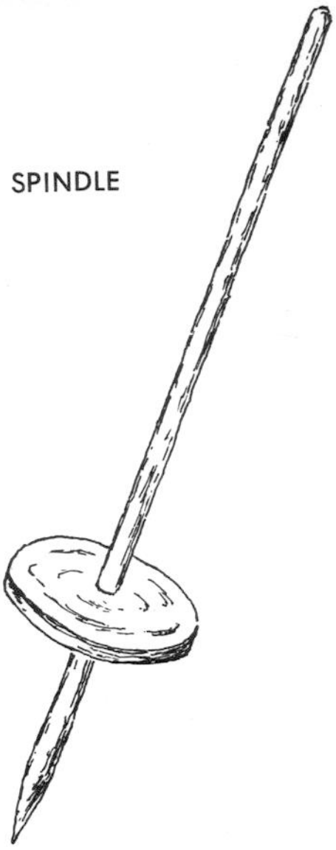

9. LOOM. A-Lower loom bar. B-Upper loom bar. C-Tension beam. D-Upper beam. E-Suspension cord. F-Tension cord. G-Loom strings. H-Lower beam. I-Border cord. J-Warp. K-Selvage cords.

H. Langley

the end of the starter thread causes the line of yarn to grow in length. Twirl, stretch, jerk, twirl, stretch, jerk—over and over the process is repeated, adding more rolls of carded wool until all of the wool is twisted into thread. More wool is used in the first spinning to make it heavier and coarser for the warp. Additional spinnings, pulling and twisting the original yarn into finer and finer thread, is used for the weft. (Photo 9) An interesting sidelight: because the yarn is held in the left hand, the Navajo home-spun has a left-hand twist. Pueblo yarn and practically all machine-made yarns have a right-hand twist.

If the yarn is to be dyed, that process takes place after the spinning.

No modern innovations appear in the Navajo vertical loom. The frame and all other parts are used as long as they serve their intended function—some looms have been used for generations. Navajos, as all good craftsmen, hate to sell the tools they have become accustomed to using, no matter how simple. New tools are made for sale, as are sample looms—set up and bearing partially woven rugs.

The first yarn to be placed on the loom is the warp thread, this is strung between the upper and lower loom bars. The down-thread crossing behind one or the other of the bars, the up-thread running opposite, so that the closely placed threads form a figure eight crossing in the middle. (Photo 9)

After the warps are strung, strong border cords—top and bottom—are woven into place. These serve primarily to keep the warp threads separated and in place.

The weaver of a simple, over-and-under tapestry weave rug will use two heddle rods—one tied to alternating warp threads, the other—a loose untied heddle—is inserted between the other warp threads. This latter heddle is used to pull forward the even warp threads. Thus by pulling one heddle, all even numbered warps are brought forward and separated from the odd numbered ones. These threads are held apart by insertion of a batten (an 18 to 24-inch flat wood piece). Between the sheds thus created, the weft threads the part of the rug you see are placed. These weft threads are combed into place with a wooden toothed comb, then tamped down into place with the batten.

Weaving a rug—as you can see—can be a lot of work. From time to time we hear reports that a Navajo weaver is poorly paid, maybe an average of 5 cents or so an hour, for her labor. Unfortunately, there is much truth to this, but it should be pointed out that rug weaving is a spare-time avocation.

A dealer friend of mine once placed an expert Navajo weaver on his payroll at $1 an hour. For her he bought hand-spun vegetal dye yarns. He told the woman to do two pieces of weaving: a better than average, twill weave, double saddle blanket (30x60 inches), and a 3x5 foot quality rug. The saddle blanket was completed in 140 hours, the rug in 238 hours! And this, I would remind you was straight weaving time—not spare time.

If this weaver had shorn, washed, carded, spun and dyed her own wool, my friend conservatively estimates that it would have taken another 200 hours.

The two pieces of weaving were sold at the going market price (in 1955) of $35 for the saddle blanket and $65 for the rug. This compares with the $140 which my friend paid for the saddle blanket and the $238 which he paid for the 3x5 foot quality rug. Which brings up a very important point: although weaving is an essential part of the reservation economy it is not exercised as a full-time occupation. Hence there can be no wage scale. A Navajo woman will do most of her weaving in her spare time, as some of our non-Indian ladies will knit a wool dress in their spare time.

CHAPTER THREE —

RUG TYPES AND AREAS

No two Navajo rugs are exactly alike; however, even the budding expert can trace (usually at a glance) many rugs to their place of origin. This is possible because certain trading post centers produce rugs of distinctive style, pattern and color. You need not be an architect to know that a shingled white frame house with shuttered windows and a sharp-pitched roof belongs to Cape Cod, not in a Los Angeles suburb. By the same token, you need not be a Navajo textile expert to know that black, white, gray and brown geometrically-designed rugs are woven in the Two Gray Hills area (and in the rug fancier's jargon, are known simply as "Two Gray Hills").

The Reservation can be divided into 13 weaving regions, each producing a characteristic rug. But, before you embark on this *Short Course in Navajo Rug Types,* constantly bear in mind, the disconcerting fact that sometimes—though, blessedly, rarely —someone will put up a Cape Cod style house in Southern California. (See Map of the Reservation).

1. Shiprock-Red Rocks Area

Beginning in the northeast corner of the reservation, the first rug to be studied here is the Shiprock-Red Rocks type. Shiprock, that massive volcanic plug around which this weaving type centers, is one of the Southwest's most famous landmarks. The San Juan River, a migrant desert stream, cuts through this valley on its west-bound course to the Colorado River.

In the early part of this century, the so-called Yei Blanket was commercially developed by Will Evans, one-time trader-owner of the Shiprock Trading Company.

The Yei is a religious figure taken from the highly stylized sandpaintings, and is their actual representation of these super-natural beings. But, while this blanket's central design is depicted in healing rites and designs reverently made by medicine men, the typical Yei Blanket itself has no religious significance. (Photo 20).

This is not to say that the old Navajos did not at first object to the weaving of sacred figures into these blankets—they protested violently and vehemently. But Will Evans' insistence quickly buried the opposition along with the taboo. Never was there an attempt by the Navajos to pass off these blankets as sacred, and because such rugs were never a part of Navajo ceremonials, the conflict died aborning. The Yei should not be confused with the so-called Ceremonial or Prayer rugs, which are strictly a product of the white-man's over-trained commercial mind; nor with the Sandpainting rug, discussed in a later chapter. There is no such thing as a prayer rug in Navajo textile arts. The Navajos do not pray on a special rug in the style of the Mohammedans. Actually, "prayer rug" and "ceremonial rug" are misnomers sometimes used as a sales pitch to the uninitiated.

The Shiprock-Red Rocks Yei usually carries a white background—for good and sufficient reason: the Yei figures are quite colorful. I have seen Yeis adorned in as many as 15 shades and hues. In addition to their brightly costumed slender figures on white backgrounds, the typical Yei blanket has a third characteristic: a stylized rainbow figure woven down its two sides and across the bottom. (Photo 13).

A Yei usually tends to be on the small size. In fact, a 3x5 Yei is considered a big rug. I think the subject matter, which lends itself to a wall-hanging type of tapestry, dictates, in turn, the relatively small size of this rug. Rarely will the average home take an oil painting larger than 3x5 feet in size, and in the best sense of the word, a good Yei is a fine painting.

The trend is toward use of more commercial, less hand-spun wool, in the Yei Blanket. Today the ratio is an even 50-50. (For comparative prices, see chart, page 65. All references to this price chart will be indicated by the use of (*).)

Less common than the Yei is the rug known as a Yeibichai. (Photo 21). The difference between the two is simple but pronounced: while the Yei is a slender-figured diety, the Yeibichai represents a line of Navajo dancers impersonating Yeis. They are delineated in human form. The Yei blanket seldom has a border; the Yeibichai seldom is without one. As a rule, the Yeibichai is a more expensive rug. (*)

Is the Shiprock-Red Rocks area the *only* place where the Yei and Yeibichai rugs are woven? No. Does this then explain why it is not uncommon to see the dancing god blanket in most all trading posts on the Reservation? Again the answer is no, and in this seeming contradiction we have an important clue to one of the idiosyncracies of the Navajo rug business.

In the first place, I would guess that 80 to 90 percent of all Yei Blankets are woven in the Shiprock-Red Rocks area. But the Yei—as with all other distinctive types of rugs—has a habit of *walking out* of a trading post. The weaver, recognizing the value of a relatively rare type of rug, will be more prone to try for a higher price than the one offered by the neighborhood trader. And so, if the San Juan Valley trader's final offer is not acceptable, the weaver will gather up her rug and walk out, and take a ride to Gallup or Farmington or even farther. So distinctive is the Yei, the fancier immediately recognizes it as a Shiprock-Red Rocks type, no matter where the far-ranging family pick-up truck finally delivers its goods.

2. Lukachukai Area

West of the Lukachukai Mountains lies the triangle of trading posts—Upper Greasewood, Round Rock and Lukachukai—that deal with a unique rug type bearing the latter post's name.

From over the mountains came the Yei design, but if the Shiprock-Red Rocks Yei tapestry is a fine portrait suitable for wall display, the Lukachukai Yei is quite content to take its place on the floor. In fact, the Lukachukai Yei is a rather heavy floor rug, for only handspun wool goes into its production.

The coarse floor Yeis are also stylized representations of Yei figures, but these Yeis, not as fussy as their Shiprock relations, repose on gray, red or black backgrounds as well as on white. There seems to be no reluctance on the part of the weaver to hold back on the reds when it comes to choosing a color for the Yeis themselves.

The usual size for a Lukachukai Yei is from 3 x 5 to 4 x 6 feet. Occasionally a weaver will try for some sort of local record, and a large rug will emerge. I have seen Lukachukai Yeis 8 x 10 feet in size, which means the Yei figures are tall as men. The weavers in this area also make good aniline dye rugs in the regular patterns in red, gray, black and white. (*)

3. Teec Nos Pos Area

West of Shiprock, near the common boundary point of Arizona, New Mexico, Colorado and Utah, is Teec Nos Pos (Circle of Cottonwood Trees). Today, a paved road links this post with the outside world, but it has been only a matter of months since the dusty, bumpy journey to Teec Nos Pos was an adventure meriting the most serious preparation. Actually there are two main posts in the weaving area at the north end of the Carrizo Mountains: Teec No Pos itself, and Beclabito (Water Under a Ledge).

The Teec Nos Pos rug is at once the most distinctive and least "Navajo" of all the Reservation's specialized textile types. It is also the hardest rug to place in a home—not because of its non-Indian characteristic, but because of its complexity of design and abundance and variety of color are hard to fit into the average home's decoration scheme. The Teec Nos Pos reserves its greatest appeal for the serious collector. (Photo 10).

10. TEEC NOS POS RUG. All colors aniline dyed handspun. Made in 1950. UNM-MC.

The distinctive rug from Teec Nos Pos features an outline design. That is, every band, diamond, bar, stripe, square or slash is outlined in one or more different colors and the design areas are filled with color. Characteristically, these rugs are very "busy". The main theme is usually a serrated zig zag. (Photo 22).

Some of nature's rainbows would be hard-pressed to show the colors of a Teec Nos Pos Outline: the more common reds, blacks, whites and grays are joined in unabashed concert with yellows, greens, purples, oranges and florescent pinks.

Where did all of this come from? My guess is a forgotten but resourceful trader showed his best Navajo weavers sketches of the type of rug designs then (early 1900s) in vogue with Eastern U.S. homemakers. These designs could have come from sketches of rugs originating in Northern Persia. Some sources credit a Mrs. Wilson (given name, occupation and home address unknown) with having encouraged the San Juan Valley weavers how to use the outline design.

Today's Teec Nos Pos outline is principally produced of commercial yarns. They vary in size from 3 x 5 up to 6 x 9 feet (*). However, the largest one I ever saw measured 10 x 18 feet. An interesting feature of this rug was the weaver's name woven into the center.

4. Red Mesa Area

West and slightly north of Teec Nos Pos, hard against the Utah border, are a trio of trading posts—Red Mesa, Sweetwater and Mexican Water—where a group of weavers are producing distinctive rugs. Usually made of handspun yarn, the Red Mesa area rugs have a coarse finish, but are of good quality. The geometric patterns are done in the traditional reds, grays, blacks and whites—but here and there in a rug will be a bar of blue or a slash of green, or both.

Some of these weavers outline their designs in the tradition of the Teec Nos Pos, but the Red Mesa rugs lack the gaudy colors of the Teec Nos Pos rugs (Photo 23).

The sizes vary from 3 x 5 to 8 x 10 feet. (*)

5. Two Gray Hills Area

Square foot for square foot, the Two Gray Hills is the finest rug that has come—and continues to come—from the post-Classic Navajo loom.

The Two Gray Hills post, along with the neighboring posts of Brinks (at Newcomb) and Toadlena (which means "water bubbling out of the ground"), are west of U.S. Highway 666 midway between Shiprock and Gallup. Toadlena is at the foot of the Chuska Mountains; Two Gray Hills is on the plain, and Brinks is on the highway.

Two competing traders, George Bloomfield and Ed Davies, deserve the credit for the eminence enjoyed by the Two Gray Hills—the Aristocrat of Navajo Rugs.

Davies, an Englishman, arrived on the scene at Two Gray Hills in 1909. Soon after, Bloomfield, a devout Mormon, set up shop at Toadlena, a scant five miles from Two Gray Hills. The two men soon became fast friends.

Before the arrival of Davies and Bloomfield, the Two Gray Hills rug was of ordinary quality and undistinguished design. (See Photo 11 for a picture of the 1911 Shiprock Fair showing the original type of rugs from this area.) In the space of 15 years, Two Gray Hills was the best as far as fine spun yarn is concerned, and it has never been topped in this.

These two dedicated traders achieved this by long, patient hours on their knees—not praying—but going over every stitch of rug with its weaver, complimenting the fine points, kindly urging improvement where improvement was called for. In the best Indian trader tradition, Davies and Bloomfield and their weavers developed a fine art form out of the nondescript craft that they inherited in this area.

What did they build on? A rug woven of natural color blacks, whites, grays and shades of browns—still the distinguishing colors of the Two Gray Hills rugs. For gray, the black and

11. SHIPROCK FAIR, 1911. It should be noted that there are no designs shown here that resemble the Two Gray Hills of today.

12 .TWO GRAY HILLS TAPESTRY WEAVE. Handspun native wool. Woven by Bessie Many Goats, Toadlena, 1945. Author's collection.

white are carded together; for tan, brown and white are blended. The traders learned early that the Navajos in the Two Gray Hills area—unlike all other Navajos in this respect—have no affection for the color red, either in their dress or in their rugs. The basic Two Gray Hills pattern remains unchanged: geometric designs. (Photo 12). There is a common belief that the old type Crystal area rug weaver's designs filtered over the mountains to influence the Two Gray Hills craftswomen, but the evidence for this is far from conclusive.[18]

For Bloomfield and Davies, it was a long, hard pull, but by 1925 they were buying and selling fine rugs of distinctive workmanship, color and design. The blacks, whites, grays and browns were now being woven into sophisticated patterns—small geometric groupings balanced in the final symmetrical whole. The Two Gray Hills rug is also characterized by a black border. It can be said of this rug that the 4 x 6 foot size is pretty much standard.

If the Two Gray Hills is, square foot for square foot, the finest rug coming off the Navajo looms today, then it follows that it is also the most expensive.[19] A small Two Gray Hills (less than 3 x 5 feet) will cost at least $100. A small tapestry of the finest weaves—the kind you display under glass—recently sold for $2000. (*)

Daisy Togelchee of Toadlena is without doubt in my estimation, the greatest living Navajo weaver. A good Navajo rug may have 30 weft threads to the inch—Mrs. Togelchee will average 100 weft threads, and some of her work has an astounding 115 weft threads to the inch!

6. Crystal Area

While Davies and Bloomfield had success in obtaining high standards at Two Gray Hills, it should be pointed out that their achievement was not without precedent. South and west of Two Gray Hills and beyond Washington Pass is the post of Crystal, where J. B. Moore held sway from 1896 to 1911. Moore realized the rugs then coming out of the Reservation needed drastic upgrading in both workmanship and design. The Eastern market had preconceived ideas of what Indian designs should be. They possibly were influenced by the beadwork patterns and colors. So the designs were altered to make them more acceptable to the white buyers.

Washington Pass is closed in the winter, but in pre-automobile days, Crystal was almost as isolated in the more benign seasons as it was in the harsh winter. In this remote proving-ground, Moore set out to develop the popular Crystal rug. "Our first thought" he wrote, ". . . to to get them to weave for us . . . all the fine rugs they can . . ."[20]

To promote weaving, Moore published a handsome catalog in 1911 (featuring the first color plates of Navajo rugs) for the

By permission Sim Schwemberger.

NAVAJO RUG IN THE MAKING.
Weaver at work.

The weaver's fancy being the governing factor in all this class of work, there is a much wider range of sizes as well as quality in it, and there is no such thing as standardizing it. It does happen at times that we have patterns and sizes as desired in it and are glad to send them when we have. But more often we have not, and the best we can do is to substitute the nearest we may have and let it go at that. No certain size in a certain pattern can be promised.

Some of the rugs are very fine and beautiful, but not all are, and some are anything but nice and handsome. Sizes may be said to run from 3x5 feet up to 5x8 feet with some both larger and smaller.

Prices — Are here a much more difficult problem than in the "ER-20" class, where all are uniformly fine. The old way, when all Navajo rugs were of uniformly poor quality, was to sell per lb. of weight, and for a goodly portion of this grade it is yet perhaps as good a way as any. The very reasonable objection to this weight basis is, that no one who buys rugs on it can quite escape buying along with them a percentage of dirt and grease, and the less he pays per lb. the greater the percentage, and the less real rug he gets in proportion. On the other hand, the seller can hardly set a price on such basis that will bring him or the weaver an adequate return on the best work of the grade, and in the extra fine ones, he HAS to come to the price per piece in the end.

Yet, there are still those who insist on pound quotations and I give them here as follows:

Coarse and common weaves, ordinary hand-washed wool, color and pattern work, heavy in proportion to size, all sizes, at $1.00 per lb.

Better quality weave, cleaner, better colors and patterns, lighter weights in proportion to size, at $1.25 per lb.

Fine, firm and solid weaves, very well cleaned, good colors and patterns, very durable, at $1.50 per lb.

Very fine weave, and nearly perfectly clean, finest colors and patterns, all sizes, at up to $2.00 per lb., according to quality.

13. PAGE FROM J. B. MOORE'S CATALOG, 1911.
Note mention of Pound Blankets.

14. GALLUP THROW. About 18" x 34". Cotton warp,
aniline dyed handspun weft.

mail order buyer. In this now rare booklet, he described the Crystal rugs and told his customers how they could order same through the mail—at the top price of $1 per square foot of rug! (Photo 13).

Quality, and its resulting higher earnings for both trader and weaver, steadily mounted until the Crystal rug was distinctive and highly marketable.

The early Crystals were 20 percent Navajo design and 80 percent Moore's conception of what Navajo design should be to be saleable. He did not hesitate to draw from his own imagination when other sources were dried up. These rugs had borders, crosses, diamonds and a characteristic hook figure somewhat resembling the letter "G" lying on its side. (Photo 24). The weavers knew a good thing, and they hewed to the Moore line, turning out rug after rug in the handsome Crystal mode.

Moore seemed to enjoy red as much as his Two Gray Hills neighbors detested it. After all, *his* customers expected red in their rugs. Red is much in evidence, along with the natural blacks, white, grays and browns, in the Moore-period Crystals. While there was definite improvement in design and color scheme the early Crystal was a good seller because the trader insisted on good weaving with clean, well-spun wool.

After Moore took his leave of the Reservation, the quality and distinctiveness of the Crystal rug followed hard on his heels.

By the time the Two Gray Hills rug was coming into flower, the classic Crystal was dead.

Yet, out of the ashes emerged a new Crystal type, dating from the 1940s. This rug is as serviceable and distinctive as its predecessor, but today's Crystal departs radically in two important respects.

The modern Crystal features vegetal dyes (of which more later) —rich tawny colors in the brown-yellow-tan-orange range— with a touch of black and subtle green. Sometimes aniline dyes are used in combination with these vegetal dyes. Master weaver Desbah Nez was the first woman at Crystal to use vegetal dyes— this, around 1940.

The second difference is in design. Today's Crystal is banded—either in straight or wavy lines. This is a sharp departure from the old style rugs produced here, and it can be stated without equivocation that the modern Crystal is the most simple of all the Navajo contemporary design types. (Photos 25 and 26).

Handspun yarns are used, even today, in this weaving center, which means a modern Crystal tends to be on the heavy side, thus making it particularly well suited for floor duty.

Crystals, as do other rugs, vary from 3 x 5 to 8 x 10 feet. Larger rugs are made and some almost square rugs come from here. (*)

7. Gallup Area

Continuing south we come to the city of Gallup, a center for the inexpensive rug known as a "Throw". While rugs are brought into Gallup from all corners of the Reservation, the distinctive Gallup weaving is made with cotton warp and is usually a small 18 x 35 inches in size. The warp is usually left loose at the ends and knots are tied close to the last weft, to make a fringe two to three inches long.

These rugs are not designed to take much abuse, and therefore see most of their service as decorative table top covers, chair backs and pillow tops. The finer throws are sometimes displayed on walls.

The Gallup Throw should not be referred to as a "single saddle blanket". The average Throw is too small and lightweight to be of much use either over or under a saddle. This is not to say Navajo rugs do not see service as saddle blankets, rather, the distinctive Gallup type being considered here is not primarily intended for use on a horse or on the floor. (See photo 14).

The Gallup Throw has no distinctive pattern, design or color. Even rudimentary Yei figures and corn stalk patterns crop up on these pieces of weaving. Although more often than not these Yeis are crudely done, such Throws will command a slightly higher price. You can buy Throws for under $10.

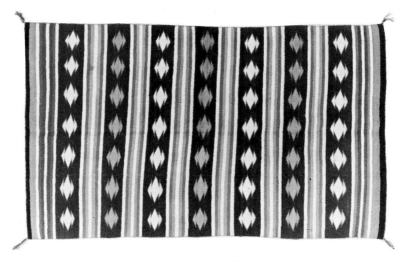

15. CHINLE RUG. Borderless. All colors aniline dyed. Prices' All-Indian Shop, Albuquerque, N.M.

16. STORM PATTERN, as shown in Moore's 1911 catalog. UNM-MC.

8. Chinle Area

Flanked by the Black Mountains to the west and the Chuska Mountains to the east, is the long valley of Chinle (pronounced chin-lee, and means "At the Mouth of the Canyon," in this case, Canyon de Chelley). The principal trading posts are Garcia's, Chinle Valley, Red Bluffs (formerly Many Farms), Nazlini and Thunderbird.

The Chinle Rug is distinctive, but it may take some doing to tell it apart from a Main Vegetal Dye specimen, which I shall describe in Section 9. Suffice it to say that a Chinle is a rug of all-vegetal, or part vegetal and part aniline dye, whose design is strongly reminiscent of the old borderless blanket. The simple Chinle motif—stripes and bands embellished with serrated designs —are carried out in the subtle vegetal pastel hues, but generally darker than the other vegetal dyes, they even include a khaki color. (Photo 15).

While a good general rug is produced in the Chinle area it should be pointed out that the distinctive Chinle does not have as fine a weave as the Wide Ruins Area rugs. Mention should be made here, also, that vegetal dye Yei rugs are made in the Chinle area. (*)

9. Wide Ruins Area

This is the *main* Vegetal Dye area. Amid the cedars in the higher elevations south of Chinle Valley are the trading posts of Klagetoh ("Cloudy or Dirty Water"), Wide Ruins, Pine Springs and Burnt Water. From this area come the best examples of the vegetal dye technique, the most important and far-reaching *modern* innovation in Navajo textile art.

Are you surprised to learn that the use of an abundance of native dyes in yarn is something new on the Reservation? Don't be, for the person directly responsible for reviving this "lost" technique was surprised, too!

On page 436 of the fourth Schoolcraft volume published in 1854, we read: "The colors which are given in the (Navajo) yarn are red, black and blue. The brightest red by . . . strips of Spanish (bayeta) cochineal dyed goods which have been purchased in the towns."[21]

No hint here of vegetal dyes, other than the fact that the blue came from indigo plant crystals imported from Mexico.

Matthews makes the only mention of vegetal dyes to be found in the early reference works, and he hardly described a galaxy of colors.[22] He tells of native dyes in the shades of "yellow, reddish and black." The yellow from rabbit brush; black from sumac, piñon pitch and ochre, reddish from the root of mountain mahogany. Natural black wool has a reddish-brown cast and the weavers probably felt a need (as they do today at Two Gray Hills and other centers where a great deal of natural blacks are

(Text continued on Page 43)

17. NAVAJO RUG, "EYE DAZZLER" TYPE. Red is mixture of aniline dyed handspun and raveled Bayeta, blue is Indigo dye, green and yellow are aniline dyes. Purchased in Farmington, N.M., in 1895 by E. H. Morris family. Circa 1880. UNM-MC.

18. GERMANTOWN, MAN'S WEARING BLANKET. All colors are 4-ply Germantown yarn. Circa 1885. Purchased from Erich Kohlberg. UNM-MC.

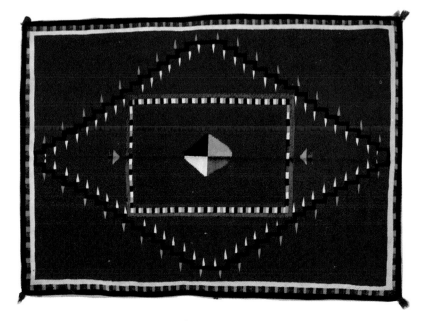

19. GERMANTOWN, MAN'S WEARING BLANKET.
Red is Germantown yarn, with the 2-ply used as
4-ply. Blue is Indigo dye. A classic design. Circa
1885. Purchased from the Fred Harvey Collection.
UNM-MC.

20 YEI BLANKET. All colors are aniline dyed handspun. Makes a good wall hanging. Purchased new
in 1957 from Don Watson Collection, Cortez, Colorado. UNM-MC.

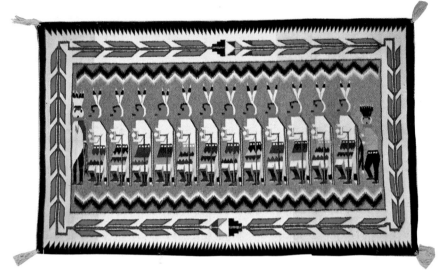

21. YEIBICHAI RUG. All colors aniline dyed hand-spun. Made by Mrs. Tom Peshlakai, Shiprock, 1956. UNM-MC.

22. TEEC NOS POS OUTLINE. Aniline dyed handspun with some commercial 4-ply yarn. Made 1956. UNM-MC.

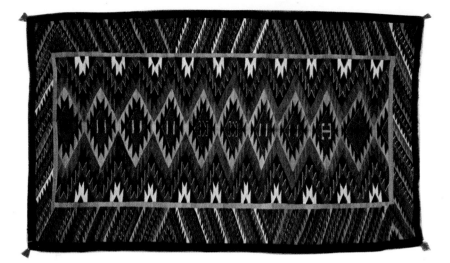

23. RED MESA OUTLINE. All colors aniline dyed handspun. Purchased by Olson family of Farmington, N.M., in 1910 and used in their home until 1956. UNM-MC.

24. OLD STYLE CRYSTAL. Red is aniline dyed handspun. Purchased in 1915, by an Iowa family, from the old J.B. Moore Catalog.

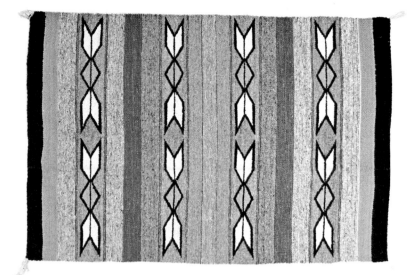

25. CONTEMPORARY CRYSTAL. All colors native handspun, vegetal dyed. Excellent floor rug. Made 1959. Author's Collection.

26. CONTEMPORARY CRYSTAL. All colors native handspun, vegetal dyed. Excellent floor rug. Prices' All-Indian Shop, Albuquerque, N.M.

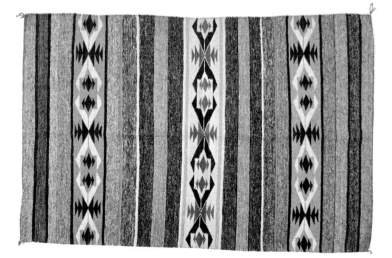

27. VEGETAL DYE RUG. Typical borderless rug, with striped designs, from the Klagetoh - Wide Ruins area. Prices' All-Indian Shop, Albuquerque, N.M.

28. GANADO TYPE RUG. Red in aniline dyed. All yarn is native handspun. Made 1951. Author's Collection.

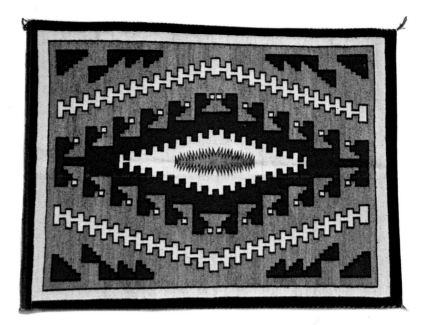

29. KLAGETOH TYPE RUG. Red is aniline dyed. Natural grey background. All handspun. Excellent floor rug, made in 1957. Author's Collection.

30. SUNRISE-KLAGETOH TYPE RUG. Red is aniline dyed. All yarn is hand spun. Excellent floor rug. Made 1955. Author's Collection.

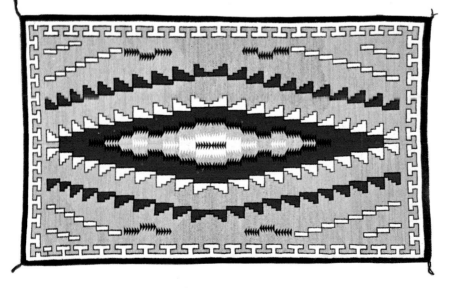

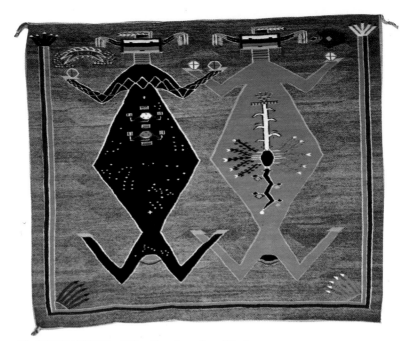

31. SANDPAINTING RUG. Showing the "Mother Earth and Father Sky" design from one of their sacred chants. All colors are aniline dyed handspun. Made 1959. UNM-MC.

32. PICTORIAL RUG. All colors are aniline dyed handspun. Woven at Lukachukai, Arizona, 1961. UNM-MC.

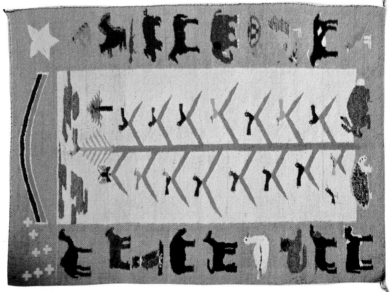

33. TWO-FACED RUG. Native handspun, aniline dye.
Purchased from Fred Harvey Co., 1946. UNM-MC.

34. CLASSIC BLANKET. A child's wearing blanket.
Excellent example of the Classic Period weaving.
Red is raveled Bayeta and 3-ply Saxony yarn. Blue
is indigo dyed. Circa 1860. Purchased from the
Clay Lockett Collection. UNM-MC.

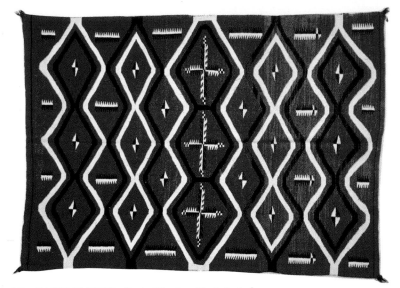

35. CLASSIC BLANKET. Man's Wearing Blanket. Red is raveled Bayeta and 3-ply Saxony yarn. Blue is Indigo dyed. Balance is handspun. Fine example of the Classic Period. Obtained from the Alfred Barton Collection. UNM-MC.

36. CLASSIC BLANKET. Man's Wearing Blanket. Red is raveled Bayeta. Blue is Indigo dyed, balance is handspun. Good example of the Classic Period. Circa 1870. Obtained from the F. H. Douglas Collection. UNM-MC.

used) to intensify the black with vegetal or other dyes. The red was extracted, primarily, to dye moccasins. Mountain mahogany's red is decidedly on the soft reddish-brown side.

George Pepper, writing on Navajo dyes in 1903[23] mentions these same three (but no new) vegetal colors. Both of these authorities *assumed* the Navajos achieved a fourth color—light green—by mixing yellow with indigo.

I have never seen a pre-1890 blanket containing actual red vegetal dye, and only a very few with a yellow dye.

As we learned earlier, Navajo weaving went into a decline around 1890, the slump lasting 30 years. In the early 1920s at Thunderbird Ranch in Chinle, two good friends of the Navajo decided to see what they could do to reverse this dismal trend. It was their feeling that the weavers had to strike some sort of compromise between the gaudy aniline dye rug and the rather sombre black-white-gray-brown natural color rug which was then coming into its own at Two Gray Hills. The answer, they felt, was a rug that was colorful but at the same time subtle—in a word: pastel.

L. H. "Cozy" McSparron, Navajo trader and Mary Cabot Wheelright, Navajo benefactress, launched experiments in co-operation with the Dupont Chemical Company. Their combined purpose was to develop commercial dyes that matched the soft but rich shadings so much in evidence in the Indian's environment.

It was a good and noble idea, but it didn't work because the Dupont dyes had to be fixed with acids—a hazardous and painstaking procedure which was felt to be too dangerous and involved to leave in the hands of the unskilled Indian. As it turned out, Cozy had to do all of the mixing himself—and that sort of thing could not go on too long.

If Cozy and Miss Wheelright were frustrated in the creation of new colors, they had better luck with design. They succeeded in reviving the old blanket styles in a good floor rug. The weavers began producing borderless rugs with simple stripes and bands of patterns—with the usual and inevitable variations. The vegetal design is relegated and confined to bands rather than spread throughout the rug in an overall design. (Photo 27)

The real development of vegetal dyes began in 1930 with the work of Nonabah G. Bryan, a Navajo woman employed as a weaving teacher at the Wingate Vocational High School.

Mrs. Bryan experimented with vegetal dyes, preparing recipes for them. She used plant materials from the far corners of the Reservation, and was successful in creating 84 different dyes. Mrs. Bryan's daughter, Mrs. Kennie Begay, recalls how as a child she tramped "over every hill in Navajoland" collecting plant materials with her mother. Mabel Burnside Myers, an early student of Mrs. Bryan's, is still active in vegetal dye work and has herself developed approximately 50 *new* colors, plus many variations by combining these colors.

Despite the foreword to a booklet published on Mrs. Bryan's work in 1940 ". . . recognizing the unique achievements of these ancient art-craftsmen and desiring to perpetuate their art, the . . . Wingate Vocational High School undertook in 1934 and 1935 to revive interest in native dyed rugs by discovering how these native dyes were obtained . . ."[24] this industrious woman's achievements were in the main completely original.

Eighty-four beautiful pastel shades! As for instance; from the cliff rose, a dye that turns wool a golden hue. "2 pounds of fresh cliff rose, twigs and leaves; ¼ cup raw alum; 1 pound of yarn. Boil the twigs and leaves in 5 gallons of water for 2 hours. Strain. Add raw alum to the dyewater. Stir and let boil 10 minutes. Add the wet yarn and stir again. Boil for 2 hours. Allow to remain in the dyebath overnight. Rinse." From alder: soft brown or tan, depending on intensity. From bee plant: greenish yellow and mustard. From prickly pear cactus: rose and pink. From ironwood: light gray. From sagebrush: greenish yellow, and so on—all is detailed in Mrs. Bryan's remarkable booklet.[25]

Much of the credit for the high quality of the vegetal dye rug belongs to Sally and Bill Lippincott, who purchased the Wide Ruins Trading Post in 1938. The Lippincotts encouraged weavers to up-grade their products, with good results. Today's vegetals are all hand-spun and feature a fine weave. Some natural gray and white are used—but no aniline dye. (*)

There is an unfortunate footnote to the success enjoyed by vegetal dye rugs. Weavers in nearby areas, skilled in the production of good red-black-gray-white rugs (The Ganado rug, Section 10) lately have taken up vegetal dye weaving with less than rousing success. This may be due to a conflict of design and color, or lack of knowledge in the use of vegetal dyes. (*)

10. Ganado Area

Between Chinle and the area of the vegetal dye rugs lies Ganado, famed headquarters of the greatest of all traders, J. Lorenzo Hubbell, and home of the traditional and most distinguished red-black-white-gray rug. (Photo 28).

As is to be expected, there is considerable over-lapping in Reservation weaving domains. Thus, Klagetoh Trading Post is noted for both its vegetals and its Ganado types. (Photo 29). This latter rug also finds its way into the posts at Lower Greasewood and Sunrise. (Photo 30).

The Ganado is perhaps the most "familiar of all" Navajo rugs. It comes closest to what most people think a Navajo rug should look like, that is—strong geometric patterns, bold and clean cut, with good solid colors.

For this we must credit the fertile brain of Don Lorenzo—and the business savvy of the Fred Harvey Company, which purchased thousands of dollars worth of red-black-white-gray rugs from the Hubbell post and sold them to tourists up and down the railroad line.

Hubbell's taste directly influenced the Ganado. He didn't like a wild array of colors, and resisted the use of aniline dyes—except for red, of which he seems to have been very fond. A beautiful dark red characterizes the Ganado, and I rather suspect Don Lorenzo urged his weavers to use a double portion of red dye. The only other aniline dye that appears in Ganado is black, used as a fortifier on natural black wool.

The average Ganado tends to be on the large size—for which we again must thank Don Lorenzo. A typical rug will have a brilliant, dark red background enclosed in a black b o r d e r , though the border is not always in evidence. The main design theme is made up of crosses and diamonds. The Ganado is somewhat uncomplicated in design, and the trend is toward more finesse and simplicity. As noted above, however, the traditional red-black-gray-white weavers are showing quite a bit of interest in vegetal dye because of the higher prices these pastel rugs command. I consider this a very unfortunate trend.

The largest Navajo rug ever made—24 x 36 feet—came from this area in the late 1920s. Four weavers worked four years on this monster, for which they received $1900. The value today is $20,000. (*)

11. Keams Canyon-Piñon Area

The Ganado influence moved west into the rolling hills and mesas of the Reservation heartland. A unique red-black-gray-white rug is created by the weavers who trade at the posts of Keams Canyon, Piñon, Indian Wells and Bita Hochee—distinctive in both size and design.

Some of the really big rugs come from this region. One I saw was 14 x 26 feet in size. The Keams Canyon-Piñon rug features big bold designs—even on the smaller rugs. The Ganado border and rich reds are much in evidence, and while it is some times impossible to distinguish one of these rugs, in a medium size, from a Ganado when the design of the former is of conventional proportions, there is no mistaking a Keams Canyon-Piñon when the weaver concentrates on traditional design size. The weaving in this area ranges from medium quality to very good. Cost is comparable to a Ganado. The larger rugs sell for $3000 to $4000. (*)

12. West Reservation Area

The bold "Storm Patterns" characterizes the West Reservation rug from Cameron, Tuba City, Kerley's Trading Post, Copper Mine Trading Post, The Gap Trading Post, Cedar Ridge Trading Post and others in this section of Navajoland. The

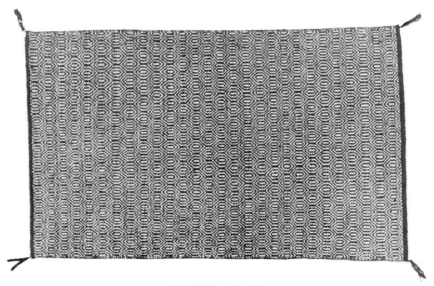

37. TWILL OR DOUBLE WEAVE. Natural wool, black, white and gray handspun. UNM-MC.

origin of the Storm Pattern is credited to a trader who operated in Tonalea around the turn of the century, and is probably as traditional as some Navajo rug designs, and more traditional than most—usually four heavy stepped lines (lightning) radiates out of a central rectangle, itself containing symbols.[26] The blocks in each of the four corners of the rug represent the four sacred mountains of the Navajos. Thus, we have a very strong rug with a single, dominant symmetrical design. (Photo 16).

The weavers here work primarily in red-black-gray-white, but there are also some very fine natural color (gray, black and white) West Reservation rugs being created today. It is safe to say, however, that a Storm Pattern rug can come in almost any color. Here the design is the distinctive feature. Here, too, the vegetal dyes have invaded the area and the results are not too good. (*)

13. Coal Mine Mesa Area

At Coal Mine Mesa and at Tuba City, a raised outline double weave rug was recently developed by a Navajo man. Ned Hatathli is responsible for this project. He was the former manager of the Navajo Arts and Crafts Guild, a Tribal Council Member and present head of the Natural Resources Committee for the Navajo Tribe. As I recall, he financed this project out of his own pocket. To my mind, this is the only really modern innovation in Navajo weaving techniques. It is a separate and distinct design and method of weaving. This shows the effect of one individual on a native craft. (*)

14. Other Distinctive Rugs

SANDPAINTING RUGS are woven copies of actual sandpaintings. (Photo 31) Weaving these sacred healing ceremony designs is still very much taboo. It takes a brave weaver to risk going blind (the proscribed fate for reproducing a sandpainting by other than in the conventional method of dry sand), but brave weavers exist.

Although a Whirling Logs sandpainting was made in the Chaco area in 1904₂₇, I have found no other mention of it until the early 1920s, when Miss Wheelright (whose work with the pastel dyes was discussed earlier), was able to persuade Hosteen Klah, a medicine man, to weave several sandpainting rugs. Also very much engaged in this project was Franc Newcomb, wife of Arthur Newcomb who operated a post in the general Two Gray Hills weaving area. The Post is now owned by Paul Brinks. (See section on Two Gray Hills, page 25).

Through Klah, many color drawings of sandpaintings were made, to serve as rug patterns. It is interesting and significant to note that today some medicine men regularly visit the Museum of Navajo Ceremonial Art in Santa Fe to study Klah's drawings on display there. Several women in the Two Gray Hills and Shiprock areas specialize in weaving authentic reproductions of these sandpaintings.

Perhaps this taboo would have broken down independent of Klah's work, but there can be no doubt that he was a pioneer.

The sandpainting rug is usually 5 x 5 feet in size— the only Navajo rug woven square on purpose. Various colors are used, and both handspun and commercial yarns. It takes a skillful weaver to copy a sandpainting, hence the price is higher than for a rug of comparable size. (*)

PICTORIAL RUGS are sort of a "Grandma Moses" thing in Navajo weaving. These are true primitives, and you are likely to find most anything depicted by the artist-weaver: birds, houses, trees, cows, horses, trains and autos. I have seen jungle animals woven into Navajo Pictorial rugs. Most Pictorials are woven in the general Lukachukai area. Not of modern origin (records indicate some Pictorial blankets were made as early as 1880), these rugs usually have a light-colored background with a wide assortment of colors used in the figures. Size of the Pictorial is usually on the small side—seldom larger than 4 x 6 and the quality of weaving is better than average. (*) (Photo 32).

Mera, in talking about Pictorial blankets says: "Quite a number of blankets, particularly some of those portraying figures were woven in black or some other somber color on a white ground.

This variety in some parts of the Southwest is popularly called a "burial blanket." It is difficult to determine how such an idea has come to be associated with blankets of this type. It may be that it relates to the well-known Navajo custom of sacrificing a horse at the grave of its owner. On the other hand, the term may perhaps have come into use through our own association of black and white with mourning. At all events, as no authentic record exists concerning the weaving of a special type of blanket for funeral purposes, the term "burial blanket" is in all probabilities quite fictitious."[28]

TWO FACE WEAVE rugs are a novelty. One side of the rug has an entirely different design than the other. To achieve this effect, the weft threads are laid one behind the other, rather than as in the conventional tapestry weave where the threads lay one atop the other. This is a difficult rug to weave and not too many are made. Two-Face weaves are not restricted to any particular area. Design, color and yarn type are as varied as the location in which you find them. (Photo 33).

SPECIAL ORDER rugs present a very difficult problem because the weaver will invariably introduce her own ideas into the design. I once commissioned a woman to weave the name and address of my business in a wall tapestry. "Farmington" came out "Framington", and the weaver was not in the least disturbed.

"Framington," she explained, "looks just as good as "Farmington." And so it does.

There is a deep lack of communication between would-be customers and weaver. If you must have your made-to-order curiosities, I suggest you either marry a weaver or learn to weave.

TWILL WEAVING (or double weaving) is a special technique usually reserved for rugs of saddle blanket size. The weaver is able to achieve many intricate designs through arrangement of the loom heddles. Some weavers will use 14 or more heddles in a single rug. The weft is allowed to skip one or more warps, depending on the pattern desired. (Photos 37 and 38).

These heavy rugs make good floor decorations. They are usually 3 x 5 feet or less in size. Twill weaving is popular in all sections of the reservation, and is used as a saddle blanket by many Navajos.

SADDLE BLANKETS. A single saddle blanket is approximately 30 inches square; a double saddle blanket measures about 30 by 60 inches. The yarn is coarsely spun, for the blanket must take rough treatment between saddle and horse's back. Saddle blankets also make marvelous floor rugs, and are quite inexpensive (at present, a single saddle blanket sells for around $11; a double for about $22). The 30 x 60 inch size is the favorite saddle blanket for Navajos. A relatively simple stripe design is most

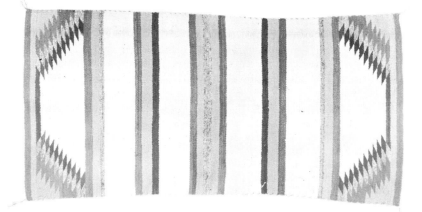

38. TWILL OR DOUBLE WEAVE. Vegetal dyed hand-spun. Purchased at Wide Ruins T.P., 1949. UNM-MC.

39. DOUBLE SADDLE BLANKET. 30" x 60". All colors aniline dyed handspun.

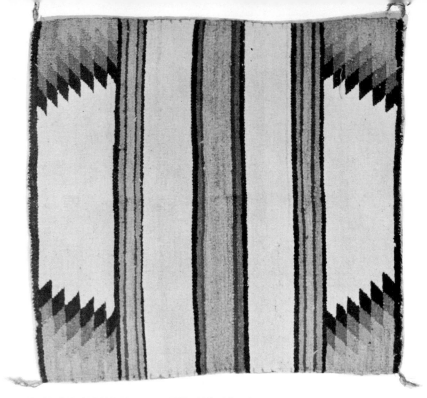

40. SINGLE SADDLE BLANKET. 30'' x 30''. All colors
aniline dyed, handspun.

41. WEDGE WEAVE. or pulled warp weave. Note
the scalloped edges caused by pulling the warp.
All colors are aniline dyed handspun. Very rare.
Circa 1890. From Earl H. Morris Collection. UNM-MC.

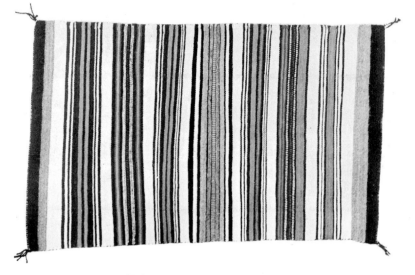

42. HOPI BLANKET. All handspun, aniline dyes.
Woven by Big Phillip, Moencopi, 1952. UNM-MC.

often used. The best examples will have corner designs that show under the skirt of the saddle. They are usually gay and gaudy, really quite colorful. (Photos 39 and 40).

Odd weaves are found, also, in saddle blankets. The most outstanding is the *Tufted Weave*. This is where the Navajo woman inserts strands of goat wool in alternate warp threads, along with her weft threads. The result is a shaggy, tufted rug, with three to four inches of wool hanging on one side, or face, of the rug. It is usually about 30 inches square.

About 50 percent of all the individual pieces of Navajo weaving made each year are saddle blankets (not counting the hand woven belts and dresses and such.) One Albuquerque dealer alone ships from 1000 to 1200 saddle blankets monthly.

SPECIALS. You will be able to find many oddities in Navajo weaving—such as pictures of Shiprock, $5, (this is the price the weaver hoped to get for her rug), letters woven into the corners, an American flag, optical illusions, and so on. These can come from any part of the reservation. Wedge weave (Photo 41) is also a special type of weave.

GENERAL RUGS—Last—but by no means least—are the blankets that do not fall into any of the above mentioned specific and distinctive rug categories. Indeed, I would estimate that each year as many General type rugs are woven as are specific-distinctive rugs, excepting saddle blankets. Thus a rough guess at production would be: 50 percent saddle blankets; 25 percent general rugs; 25 percent specific-distinctive rugs.

The General rug is the rug whose design, quality and color do not distinguish it as being from any particular locale. They may be plain stripes or geometric patterns with or without a border. Such rugs are made throughout the Reservation. Sizes vary greatly—3 x 5, 4 x 6 feet, even larger (16 x 22 feet) as do prices.

CHAPTER FOUR —

HOW TO BUY A RUG

I have noticed in my contacts with the buying public that the most important determinant of a sale is the initial impact a rug makes on the customer. A rug's size, design and color combine to produce a reaction in the buyer that seems to make him cry out: "I must have this rug!" There is no accounting for taste, and while I would be the last to advise you to buy a rug that did not appeal to you aesthetically (which you are not likely to do anyway), I would point out that there are a few helpful rules to carry into the rug buying game. These guides will aid you in making an intelligent decision. While beauty is an intangible, quality is not.

Rule Number 1: Always open up the rug being considered to its full width and length on the sales room floor. Never buy a rug of which you've seen only a half or a quarter—the folded under portion may contain serious flaws. You'll want to make sure the rug does not have built-in wrinkles. Besides, you'll want to get the rug's full visual effect.

While all Navajo rugs are "genuine" (so you need not concern yourself on that score), not all Navajo rugs are examples of quality craftsmanship.

Rule number 2: Carefully check the weave. Does the design have the same width at one end of the rug as it has at the other? Are the horizontal and vertical lines straight as well as uniform in width? Is the tightness of the weave uniform throughout the rug? Are the warp threads out of sight as they should be? No rug should or would be 100 percent perfect. Then it would look as though it were machine made and lose the charm of a hand made piece.

Rule number 3: Smoothness is an important consideration. The rug thickness should be the same throughout, with no "thin" area in a "thick" rug and vice versa.

Rule number 4: Color uniformity. A rug may suffer when a weaver is careless in dyeing her yarn. Only a relatively small amount of yarn is dyed at a time, just what she thinks will be sufficient for her rug. So, sometimes when she has to dye more for her rug, she will get marked variations in what is supposed to be a single hue. White is another color stumbing block. When wool is improperly scoured, the white will be traced with black. Dry cleaning will *not* remove these streaks. Also, check to be sure that the white yarn is not full of chalk to make it look whiter.

You should be prepared to pay more for quality weaving—but in the long run, you will not regret it. A rug is meant to be utilitarian—it is not a curio.

Navajo rugs are just one of a kind. If you like a rug and the price is right—buy it. Don't depend on the rug waiting for your return. Rug turnover is great in most retail outlets.

CHAPTER FIVE —

AFTER THE RUG IS HOME

The foregoing was intended to help you solve the problem: "What rug should I buy?" Once you pass that hurdle, you come face to face with this problem: "Now that I have the rug, what do I do with it?" Actually, there are two questions to be settled here: how to use the rug in your home, and how to care for it.

Function

Let the rug—first, last and always—be a source of personal pleasure. Put it where it pleases you most—on a bare floor, atop wall-to-wall carpeting, draped over furniture, as a car seat, or a pillow top, or on the wall. Of course, you will want to pay attention to color scheme and other decorating considerations, but you will be surprised how easily a Navajo rug will fit into most any room. I know of Navajo rugs happily at home with modern, Swedish, traditonal and even baroque period furnishings.

If you use a rug on a bare floor, I recommend you place a pad under it to keep the rug from slipping.

While the Yei, Yeibichai and tapestry weave Two Gray Hills rugs are commonly used as wall hangings, I have seen common saddle blankets hung on walls with pleasing effect. The owner loved his saddle blanket—and that is quite enough.

Care

Normal vacuum cleaning will keep a Navajo rug in good condition for years. Even an occasional cleaning with a beater-brush vacuum (Hoover, Kirby, etc.) will not reduce the rug's life expectancy. Some of the heavily used rugs in my home waited 10 years before their first trip to the dry cleaners. One tip: after each vacuuming, reverse the rug or turn end for end. This insures a uniformity of wear on both sides and ends. And too, some of the rug colors are bound to fade, especially in the bright colors. Regularly reversing a rug insures a uniform "mellowing" of color.

Never wash a rug. Small spots can be removed with commercial lighter fluid—but the over-all cleaning job is a task for an expert. If the rug needs cleaning, go to your city's finest rug dealer and ask him to recommend a dry cleaner who knows his business.

If you spill water on a Navajo rug, blot it immediately. This will prevent the improperly set native dyed yarn from running. I know of no way to erase red dye that has run over into other colors. Also remember: wool shrinks and stretches.

Any good commercial moth spray can be used on a Navajo rug. Be sure to de-moth both sides. You may want professional help in de-mothing, in which case your dry cleaner most likely can help. It is well to remember that a floor rug in constant use—and regularly reversed—is in little danger of moth damage, but rugs that are displayed on walls or stored away must definitely be protected. I would suggest that rugs to be stored are rolled, rather than folded. Wall hangings should be reversed at least twice a year as an anti-moth precaution.

Never shake-out and snap your Navajo rug. Snapping such tapestries likely will break the end cords, thus allowing the warps to come loose. If you must shake your rug, hold it by its side and gently manipulate it.

At this point let me reassure you that a Navajo rug is *not* a fragile item. An ordinary Navajo rug was placed at the entrance to the New Mexico State exhibit hall at the 1933 Chicago Century of Progress Exposition. Mud and dirt from outdoors and sand and grit from indoors was tracked across and ground into that rug by 2,800,000 pairs of careless shoes and boots—and that rug was as beautiful after the fair closed as it was on opening day. Not a single thread was broken. Depending on care and use or abuse, a Navajo rug in a home can last many years.

Any weaver can repair a small hole in a Navajo rug, but major repairs are another matter. Too often a rug owner will lose sight of the fact that most, old, beat-up Navajo rugs are simply old, beat-up rugs—period! Of course, a Classic period blanket or any other collector's item is worth saving, but usually the cost of repairing an ordinary Navajo rug will be greater than the cost of replacement, and the results less satisfactory.

I know of one or two experts in the field of repairing Navajo rugs, but they are hopelessly backlogged with work, and it would not pay you to even consider trying to deal with them.

Many rugs will turn up at one or more of their corners—and here is a repair job that you can do yourself. Simply untie the knots on the end cord (all Navajo rugs, except throws, have tasseled cords on each of the four corners). Then gently pull and loosen the cords back toward the center of the edges of the rug. After you succeed in getting the rug to lie flat, pull the excess and loose, cords back to the corners and re-tie the tassel knots.

CHAPTER SIX

HOW TO COLLECT NAVAJO WEAVING

Before you get into serious rug collecting, it will pay you to determine exactly where you want this relatively expensive hobby to take you. Will you concentrate on Old Blankets? Classic Period Blankets? Contemporary Weaves? These are the three major realms of the serious collector, and the following may help throw some light on the problems—and opportunities—presented by each of these categories.

Old Blankets

By "old" I mean anything woven prior to 1890, which will include the work of the first weavers, the pre-anilines, the "eye-dazzlers," and Classic Period Blankets (the latter is treated as a separate category below). Step number one is to visit (haunt may be a better word) the various Southwest museums: Museum of Northern Arizona in Flagstaff, Museum of Navajo Ceremonial Art in Santa Fe, Laboratory of Anthropology in Santa Fe, Heard Museum in Phoenix, University of New Mexico Museum of Anthropology in Albuquerque. All of which have outstanding collections of Navajo textiles. I would also recommend that you get on friendly terms with private collectors. Study the weaves, yarns and designs of the old textiles so you will know what to look for. It is important to *feel* as well as *see* the old rugs and blankets.

Most common error in the Old Blanket field is to confuse Germantown with Saxony and even bayeta yarn. Only long and careful study will help you over this pitfall.

For the Old Blanket collector, indigo blue is a most important color with which to become familiar. Not used after 1890, indigo is the only color employed as a dye by the old time weavers that would not fade.

As with the rug owner who unwisely goes to great expense to repair what is in truth a rug not worth salvaging, so too, the collector must guard against setting too high a value on a rug whose only good point is its age. Whiskers, *per se,* do not give value to a rug. Only one in a thousand rugs might be worth having in a collection. This singular rug is invariably a prime example of something significant, either in pattern, style or coloring, in the history of Navajo weaving.

Classic Blankets

The Classic Period of Navajo weaving, 1850-70, could be called a part of the Old Blanket Period (prior to 1890) discussed above. However, the very name "classic" gives us a clue as to why work from this period is usually placed in a class of its own. Whereas an "old blanket" woven in 1875 or 1880 may or may not be worth a place in a collection, I have seen few, if any, Classic Period Blankets *not* worth saving and showing.

The Classic is a bayeta and/or Saxony yarn blanket with white, black and indigo dyed handspun, having no border. The design theme is a simple striped motif, stepped blocks or an occasion cross. All very beautiful, all quite simple. (Photos 34, 35, and 36).

Expect to pay between $500 and $1000 for a Classic Blanket, and consider yourself extremely lucky to acquire a fine old Bayeta for less than $1000. But please remember, don't pay a high price for just an old rug. A good example: a 1963 Cadillac sells for about $6500, in 1973 it might be worth $500; a *1903* Cadillac in 1973 could very easily sell for $25,000; it is a Classic Period design in cars. But before you buy any pre-1890 blanket, Classic or otherwise, get an expert's opinion. I have seen hundreds of blankets that were mistakenly classified as pre-1880 by well-meaning and completely honest people.

Contemporary Weaves

Here you probably will want to specialize even more narrowly, concentrating on one of the specific and distinctive rug types discussed earlier. If you choose Two Gray Hills, for instance, then you'll want to become acquainted with the people at Two Gray Hills, Brinks and Toadlena, as well as the dealers who buy from these posts.

Rug collecting is a good investment—if you do not lose sight of the fact that your collection must stress, quality, *quality, QUALITY!* Good rugs—singly or in a collection—increase in value; poor rugs decrease.

CHAPTER SEVEN

FACT AND FANCY

SPIRIT TRAILS. In some rugs, especially the older ones, you will see a different colored thread running outward from the inside of the rug through the border to the selvage cord. It is commonly believed that the weavers put these spirit trails in their rugs to "let out the evil spirit." Actually, the weaver has put good spirits and ideas into her design, and when such a design in enclosed with a heavy solid border, the weaver is anxious to allow these good spirits to escape (via the spirit trail) so she can weave another good rug.

PURPOSEFUL ERRORS. Do all rugs have an error purposefully woven into them? NO! There are errors, but here we must blame the human element. Also, I think that the purposeful error idea is just a sales pitch to justify poor weaving and/or design.

PATTERNS. Because symbolic designs are not used in Navajo rugs, the weaver does not feel compelled to follow a set pattern in her design. In all my years of experience with Navajo weaving, I have seen only three pairs of matched rugs. Some of the traders may suggest a design, but what emerges is never exactly as ordered. Geometric designs are used, not because they are particularly Indian in appearance, but because of the limitation placed on design by the horizontal construction of the rug. In short, there are no pattern books for Navajo weavers. The preconceived design—if any exists before the weaver begins her work—is all in her head.

MACHINE MADE RUGS. There are no machine made Navajo rugs. There are some simple striped saddle blankets that *resemble* Navajo rugs, but the woolen mills simply cannnot copy, economically, the intricate weaving techniques used by the Navajos. On a single weft thread across the face of a typical Navajo rug there may be as many as 30 or even 50 color changes.

CHIMAYÓ BLANKETS. The Chimayó Blanket is sometimes confused with Navajo weaving. The Spanish-American weaving center at Chimayó, north of Santa Fe, New Mexico, specializes in a distinctive tapestry mostly used as bed or couch coverings. The Chimayó blanket is a light weight fabric made of commercial yarn on a horizontal, foot-operated loom, rather than a vertical loom. It has been many years since a hand-spun Chimayó was made. However, now, on these looms, the Chimayó weavers are copying the Two Gray Hills rug and the vegetal dye colorings.

MEN WEAVERS. In Navajoland, the woman is the weaver. Very rarely will a Navajo man weave. In fact, I know of only two. The situation is reversed with the Pueblos, where 99 percent of the weavers are men. Hopi weaving, exclusive tenet of the men, is practically extinct today, except for their ceremonial garments. (Photo 42).

PENDLETON BLANKET. These, the first of the machine-made blankets, hit the Reservation in 1890, and this was a main contributing factor in the decline of weaving after that date.₂₉ After all, why take the time and trouble to make a fine blanket when a commercial blanket can be purchased from the trader for a small price. Today, only Pendleton Blankets are worn (for warmth) by the Navajos. I have never seen a Navajo wearing a Navajo blanket.

CERTIFICATE OF AUTHENTICITY. In the late 1930s the Department of Interior had a brainstorm and launched a "trade-mark" program for Navajo rugs. The "certificate of genuineness for Navajo all-wool hand-woven fabrics" to "protect both the buying public and the Indian craftsman in the making and marketing of high-grade Navajo products" was fastened to rugs with wire caught in a lead seal. This practice was discontinued because it was and still is unnecessary. A hand woven Navajo rug needs no label to set it apart.

CHAPTER EIGHT —

THE FUTURE

In 1950 I purchased 3402 Navajo rugs, for which I paid a total of $69,572. This averages out to $20.42 per rug.

Ten years later, in 1960, I was only able to find 1364 rugs which I thought worthy of placing with my retail outlets. For these 1364 rugs I paid a total of $50,090. Average per rug in 1960: $36.74 (see list following.)

YEAR	NUMBER OF RUGS PURCHASED	AVERAGE PRICE PER RUG	GROSS DOLLARS
1948	3250	20.06	65,200
1949	3345	21.46	71,782
1950	3402	20.42	69,572
1951	3574	18.80	67,223
1952	3272	17.92	58,642
1953	2918	17.60	51,336
1954	3024	20.18	61,067
1955	3194	20.20	64,526
1956	1801	29.44	53,085
1957	1581	31.02	49,995
1958	1994	32.00	63,815
1959	2109	30.11	63,610
1960	1364	36.74	50,090
1961	1833	33.02	60,530
1962	1611	39.70	63,934

These are rugs, the list does not include saddle blankets.

In 1950 I used to visit the trading posts in a panel truck. It was a rare day of buying in which I did not fill that truck to capacity. (Photo 43, Maxwell rug room, 1951).

43. MAXWELL RUG ROOM, 1951

44. MAXWELL RUG ROOM, 1961

Today, I drive a station wagon, and it takes several days of running around the Reservation to get a load of rugs. (Photo 44, Maxwell rug room, 1961).

Down goes supply, up goes demand, up go prices; the universal economic fact of life.

The Navajo Reservation, remote as it is, is not immune to the simple laws that govern economics. Thus, the future of Navajo weaving is dim indeed because supply, in this case, cannot respond to increased demand and the more attractive price structure. The fine old weavers are dying off or going on relief and the young people are not learning how to weave, and who can blame them? A job in town—any job— pays more per hour than the average weaver can make in several hours. And bear in mind that the job in question need not be held by the weaver— if her husband or son start bringing home a regular paycheck she is not likely to hie herself to the loom. We no longer churn butter, whittle axe handles or weave our own cloth, even though we lament the passing of the good old days.

Recently at a Gallup filling station I chatted with a middle-aged Navajo who had come to town with his family to make purchases. His wife, a graduate of the Wingate School, quit weaving the day her husband got a job; the two daughters seated in the back of the pickup truck didn't know how to weave—and will never learn.

The native crafts are disappearing and there is no reason to believe Navajo weaving will be any different.

The art of making beautiful baskets is practically dead, as is the Plains Indian's sinew-sewn beadwork on buckskin. While some effort is being made to revive interest in Navajo weaving by teaching it in some vocational Indian schools the entire program is doomed to eventual failure because of the dollars-and-cents considerations. Simply stated, it doesn't pay to weave a Navajo rug.

"The old blankets are passing away," lamented Lorenzo Hubbell in 1902. To which, 60 years later we can sadly add: "And so is Navajo weaving." May the gods of the Navajo, who walk in beauty, grant us 60 more years!

CHAPTER NINE

RUG PRICES, 1963

This is a comparative chart and not a guide. Prices quoted are for rugs of good quality, and for 1963, *only*.

TYPE	PRICE FOR			Larger, or Specials
	3' x 5'	4' x 6'	6' x 9'	
Shiprock Yei	60 - 350			
Lukachukai	60 - 150	200 - 400	300 - 600	
Teec Nos Pos	100 - 300	150 - 500	700 - 1100	7x12 - 1500
Red Mesa	50 - 125	125 - 400	400 - 700	
Two Gray Hills	100 & up	350 & up	600 & up	Special tapestries up to 3500.00
Crystal Gallup	75 - 180	200 - 390	700 - 1000	1200 - 2000 Throws, 18" x 30" 6.00 to 8.00
Chinle	50 - 150	175 - 300	400 - 900	9' x 12' 1000 & up
Wide Ruins Area	60 & up	125 & up	300 & up	Large rugs, 1200 - 2000
Ganado	45 - 100	100 - 250	250 - 500	Up to 2500
Keams Canyon	50 - 150	150 - 290	300 - 750	1000 - 4000
West Reservation	50 - 175	125 - 250	450 - 900	900 - 1500
Coal Mine Mesa	50 - 125			
Sand Paintings	300 - 500	400 - 1000		
Pictorial	75 - 150	175 - 400		
Two-Faced	75 - 200			
Twill Weave	35 - 75			
General	40 - 100	100 - 250	250 - 800	900 & up

FOOTNOTES

1. Amsden, 1934; Underhill, 1956
2. Kupper, 1945
3. Underhill, 1953
4. Amsden, 1934; Kidder, 1920; Underhill, 1953, 1956
5. Ibid.
6. Worcester, 1951
7. Hill, 1940
8. Twitchell, 1914
9. Worcester, 1951
10. Amsden, 1934
11. Morris, 1925
12. Mera, 1948; Reichard, 1936
13. Mera, 1948
14. Underhill, 1953
15. Pepper, 1903
16. Mera, 1948
17. Underhill, 1956
18. McNitt, 1962
19. McNitt, 1959
20. Moore, 1911
21. Schoolcraft, 1854
22. Matthews, 1881-82
23. Pepper, 1903
24. Bryan, 1940
25. Ibid.
26. Hegeman, 1963
27. McNitt, 1962
28. Mera, 1948
29. Amsden, 1934
30. McNitt, 1962

BIBLIOGRAPHY

More items are listed here than are quoted in the text, but
it was felt the additional sources would be of interest to
the serious collectors.

Amsden, Charles Avery
"The Loom and its Prototypes", *American Anthropologist,* 34: 216-
235, 1932, Menasha, Wisc.

Amsden, Charles Avery
"Reviving the Navajo Blanket", *Masterkey,* 6, 137-147, 1932.

Amsden, Charles Avery
"Navajo Origins", *New Mexico Historical Review.* Vol. 7, No. 3,
pp. 193-209, Albuquerque, N.M., 1932.

Amsden, Charles Avery
Navajo Weaving. Fine Arts Press, Santa Ana, Calif., 1934.
Second Edition, University of New Mexico Press, Albuquerque,
N.M., 1949.

Backus, E.
"An Account of the Navajos of New Mexico", In Schoolcraft, H. R.
Archives of Aboriginal Knowledge, Philadelphia, 1860.

Bartlett, Katherine
"Present Trends in Weaving on the Western Navajo Reservation",
Plateau, 23:1, July, 1950.

Bloom, Lansing B.
"Early Weaving in New Mexico", *The New Mexico Historical
Review,* Vol. II, No. 3, July, 1927.

Bolton, Herbert E.
Spanish Explorations in the Southwest, 1542-1706. C. Scribner's
Sons, N.Y., 1925.

Bryan, Nonabah G., with Young, Stella
"Native Navajo Dyes", *Indian Handcraft Series,* No. 2., Education
Division, U. S. Office of Indian Affairs, Chilocco Agricultural
School, Chilocco, Oklahoma, 1940.

Colton, Mary-Russell
"Wool for our Indian Weavers—What Shall it be?", *Museum Notes,*
4:12, June, 1932.

Coolidge, Mary Roberts
The Rain Makers, Boston & New York, Houghton Mifflin Co., 1929.

Coolidge, Dane & Mary Roberts
Navajo Rugs, Esto Publishing Co., Pasadena, Calif., 1933.

Douglas, Frederic H.
Indian Leaflet Series, Nos. 3; 21; 56; 59-60; 71; 89; 92-93; 94-95;
113; 116; Denver Art Museum, Denver, Colorado.

Duclos, Antoinette S.
"Navajo Warp and Woof" *Arizona Highways Magazine,* August,
1942.

Dutton, Bertha
Navajo Weaving Today, Museum of New Mexico Press, Santa Fe,
N.M., 1961.

Elmore, Frances H.
Ethnobotany of the Navajo, Albuquerque, N.M., University of New
Mexico and School of American Research.

Forbes, Jack D.
Apache, Navajo and Spaniard. University of Oklahoma Press, Norman, 1960.

Gillmore, Frances and Wetherill, Louisa
  Traders to the Navajo, University of New Mexico Press, 1952, 2nd Edition.
Goddard, P. E.
  Indians of the Southwest, American Museum of Natural History, New York, 1931.
Grandstaff, James O.
  Wool Characteristics in Relation to Navajo Weaving, Washington, U. S. Department of Agriculture.
Hegeman, Elizabeth C.
  Navajo Trading Days, University of New Mexico Press, Albuquerque, 1963.
Hester, James J.
  Early Navajo Migrations and Acculturation in the Southwest, Museum of New Mexico Papers in Anthropology, No. 6, Museum of New Mexico Press, Santa Fe, 1963.
Hill, W. W.
  "Some Navajo Cultural Changes", *Miscellaneous Series,* Smithsonian Institution, No. 100, Washington, D.C., 1940.
Hodge, F.W.
  "The Early Navajo and Apache", *American Anthropologist,* 8: 223-240, Washington, 1895.
Hollister, Uriah S.
  The Navajo and His Blanket, Denver, Colo., 1903.
Hummel, J. J.
  The Dyeing of Textile Fabrics, London, 1885.
James, George Wharton
  Indian Blankets and Their Makers, A. C. McClurg & Co., 1920.
Jones, Courtney R.
  "Spindle-Spinning: Navajo Style", *Plateau,* 18:3, January, 1946.
Kent, Kate P.
  "The Cultivation and Weaving of Cotton in the Prehistoric Southwestern United States", *Transactions of the American Philosophical Society,* n.s. Vol. 47, pt. 2, Philadelphia, 1957.
Kent, Kate P.
  Navajo Weaving, Heard Museum of Anthropology and Primitive Art, Phoenix, Ariz., 1961.
Keur, Dorothy L.
  "A Chapter in Navajo-Pueblo Relationships", *American Antiquity,* Vol. 10, No. 1, pp 75-86, Menasha, Wisc., 1944.
Kidder, A. V.
  "Ruins of the Historic Period in the Upper San Juan Valley, New Mexico", *American Anthropologist,* n.s., 28:618-632, Menasha, Wisc., 1920.
Kissell, Mary Lois
  Indian Weaving, Exposition of Indian Tribal Arts, Introduction to American Indian Art, Part 2, No. 10, 1931.
Kluckhohn, Clyde and Spencer, Katherine
  A Bibliography of the Navajo Indians, J. J. Augustin, N.Y., 1940.
Kluckhohn, Clyde and Leighton, Dorothea
  The Navajo, Doubleday, 1962.
Kupper, Winifred
  The Golden Hoof, Knopf, N.Y., 1945.
Marriott, Alice L.
  These are the People, Thos. Y. Crowell Co., N.Y., 1948.
Matthews, Washington
  "Navajo Weavers", Bureau of American Ethnology, *Third Annual Report,* 1882, Washington, D.C.
Matthews, Washington
  "Navajo Dye Stuffs", Smithsonian Institute, *Annual Report,* 1891.
Matthews, Washington
  "A Two-Faced Navajo Blanket", *American Anthropologist,* 2:638-642, Washington, D.C., 1900.

Matthews, Washington
"The Navajo Yellow Dye", *American Anthropoligist,* 6:194, 1904.
Matthews, Washington
"The Night Chant, a Navajo Ceremony", American Museum of Natural History, *Memoirs,* 6:1, 332.
McNitt, Frank
Richard Wetherill: Anasazi, University of Oklahoma Press, Norman, 1957.
McNitt, Frank
"Two Gray Hills—America's Costliest Rugs", *New Mexico Magazine,* April, Vol. 37, No. 4, 1959.
McNitt, Frank
The Indian Traders, University of Oklahoma Press, Norman, 1962.
Mera, H. P.
Navajo Textile Arts, Laboratory of Anthropology, Santa Fe, N.M., 1948. (This book is the collection of all of Mera's pamphlets on Navajo textiles printed in the *General Series* by the Laboratory of Anthropology, Sante Fe, N.M.)
Mera, H. P.
The Alfred I. Barton Collection of Southwestern Textiles, San Vicente Foundation, Santa Fe, N.M., 1949.
Merry, E. S.
"So You Want to Buy a Navajo Rug?", *Indian Life,* Aug., Vol. 38, No. 1, pp 30-35, Gallup, 1960.
Moore, J. B.
The Navajo, Crystal, N.M., 1911.
Morris, Earl H.
"Exploring in the Canyon of Death", *National Geographic Magazine,* XLVIII, 263-300, Washington, 1925.
Pepper, George H.
"Native Navajo Dyes", *Papoose,* L:3; 1-11, 1903.
Reichard, Gladys A.
Navajo Shepherd and Weaver, J. J. Augustin, N.Y., 1936.
Sapir, Edward
"A Navajo Sand Painting Blanket", *American Anthropologist,* 32: 575-576, Washington, 1935.
Schoolcraft, Henry R.
Indian Tribes of the United States, Part IV, Philadelphia, Lippincott, Gramby & Co., 1854.
Spicer, Edward H.
Cycles of Conquest, University of Arizona Press, Tucson, Ariz., 1962.
Spiegelberg, A. F.
"Navajo Blankets", *El Palacio,* Vol. 18, nos. 10 and 11, Santa Fe, 1925.
Thomas, A. B.
Teodoro de Croix, University of Oklahoma Press, Norman, 1941.
Twitchell, Ralph E.
The History of the Occupation of New Mexico, Smithe-Brooks Co., Denver, Colo., 1909.
Twitchell, Ralph E.
The Spanish Archives of New Mexico, 2 Vols., Cedar Rapids, Iowa, 1914.
Underhill, Ruth M.
Here Come the Navajo, Haskell Institute, Lawrence, Kans., U. S. Indian Service, 1953.
Underhill, Ruth M.
Red Man's America, University of Chicago Press, Chicago, Ill., 1953.
Underhill, Ruth M.
The Navajo, University of Oklahoma Press, Norman, 1956.
Watson, Editha L.
"Navajo Rugs", *Arizona Highways Magazine,* August, 1957.

Worcester, Donald E.
    "The Navajo during the Spanish Regime in New Mexico", *New Mexico Historical Review,* 26:II: pp 101-118, Santa Fe, April, 1951.
Young, Stella, with Nonabah G. Bryan
    "Navajo Native Dyes", *Indian Handcraft Series,* No. 2, Education Division, U. S. Office of Indian Affairs, Chilocco Agricultural School, Chilocco, Oklahoma, 1940.